tartares &
Carpaccios

Recipes by Marie-Victoire Garcia
Photography by Akiko Ida

HACHETTE
illustrated

contents

CARPACCIOS

tips and tricks

Raw food: new taste sensations

The passion for natural things has reached our tables.

Nowadays, refrigeration and preserving techniques, which ensure correct temperatures and compulsory health controls, mean that raw meat and fish can be eaten safely.

Preparing a dish of raw ingredients sometimes means simply decorating it, touch by touch as a painter might. The result is a feast for your guests' eyes matching that for their palates as they discover new textures and flavors.

One word of advice: tartares and carpaccios should not be prepared several hours in advance of serving but eaten immediately.

You can, however, take time for an aperitif … accompanied by a carpaccio or tartare canapé.

Tartare

Most of us have heard of, or even seen, the traditional plate of raw red meat decorated with an egg yolk and accompanied by a variety of condiments.

Modern tartares have a new take, using a wide range of white meats, fish, shellfish, fruit, or vegetables.

Everything is still raw, cut in little cubes or chopped, and finely seasoned to enhance the special taste of each ingredient.

Carpaccio

This dish comes to us from Italy.

There is a story of the Venetian chef who served a countess (on a diet) with a plate of raw beef fillet sliced very finely. Her guests remarked on the dish's resemblance to a work by the celebrated local painter, Carpaccio.

Nowadays, carpaccio means a dish made using paper-thin slices of meat, fish, and, latterly, vegetables or fruit, all sprinkled at the last minute with a fruity oil.

The techniques

Absolutely fresh ingredients

Tartares and carpaccios have one thing in common: the ingredients must be cold and fresh, especially meat, fish, and shellfish.

Make sure, therefore, to alert your butcher or fish supplier that you intend to serve your purchases raw.

A final cold spell

Meat and fish will be easier to cut if left for some time in the refrigerator or the freezer, to firm up the flesh. The chilling time depends on the dish to be served.

A trick for carpaccio

Brush the slices of meat or fish carefully with oil so that they do not stick together.

Utensils

A mandoline

Fruit and vegetables can be sliced very rapidly and uniformly with the help of an adjustable mandoline, or one of the new microplane graters and shavers.

A long-bladed knife

It goes without saying that an electric knife will enable you to carve very fine carpaccios. If you do not have one, a well-sharpened long-bladed knife will do the trick for tartares and carpaccios. Never use a saw-toothed knife.

A swivel-blade vegetable peeler

For some vegetables (such as shaving carrots or cucumber in long strips), you will find this type of vegetable peeler so marvelous that you will not want to do without it.

Warning

This book contains dishes that are made with raw or lightly cooked eggs. These should be avoided by vulnerable people such as pregnant and nursing mothers, invalids, the elderly, babies and young children.

Beef tartare

Serves 4

1 lb beef fillet, ground
on the day of serving

1 large white onion,
chopped

2 teaspoons strong mustard

1 teaspoon Worcestershire
sauce

3 tablespoons ketchup

1 teaspoon wine vinegar

2 tablespoons olive oil

4 egg yolks, each in a
half shell

salt and freshly ground
black pepper

Chill the beef in the refrigerator for 15 minutes.

Mix together all the ingredients for the dressing.

Add the well-chilled beef and mix in well, allowing plenty of
air to get into the blend. Divide into 4 portions and shape
each into a mound. Place one mound on each plate and
make a small indentation in the top to house the egg yolk
in its half-shell. Serve immediately.

Suggestion

You could make a more exotic Asian-style tartare by adding a
garnish of chopped cilantro leaves and/or sesame seeds.

Spiced veal tartare

Serves 4

14 oz veal fillet

2 teaspoons mustard

¼ teaspoon freshly ground black pepper

¼ teaspoon Cayenne pepper

2 tablespoons lemon juice

2 tablespoons olive oil

2 teaspoons Cognac

6 tablespoons chopped flat-leaf parsley

2 tablespoons snipped chives

2 tablespoons sour cream

salt

Refrigerate the veal fillet for an hour to firm it, then cut into very small cubes.

In a bowl mix together the mustard, pepper, Cayenne pepper, lemon juice, olive oil, and Cognac. Season with salt to taste.

Add the parsley and chives and mix well.

Add the contents of the bowl to the veal and stir in well, raising the mixture to aerate it.

Divide the tartare into four portions. Put neatly onto 4 plates and add a dollop of sour cream to each.

Suggestions

If serving this tartare as an appetizer, arrange it on a bed of grated carrots or serve with other crudités.

If served as a main dish, it goes very well with sautéed potatoes.

Salmon and cilantro tartare

Serves 4

1 lb fresh salmon fillet

4 tablespoons lemon juice

2 tablespoons olive oil

1 tablespoon wine or raspberry vinegar

3 tablespoons cilantro leaves

salt and freshly ground black pepper

4 small ramekins

Freeze the salmon for 30 minutes to firm the flesh.

Slice as finely as possible.

Mix together the lemon juice, olive oil, vinegar, and cilantro leaves, reserving a few leaves for a garnish.

Add the sliced salmon to this mixture.

Divide into 4 and put into the ramekins.

To serve, unmold each ramekin onto a plate and garnish with the remaining cilantro leaves.

Suggestion

Chives or fresh dill leaves could be substituted for the cilantro.

Mackerel and chive tartare

Serves 4

4 smoked, peppered
mackerel fillets (sold
vacuum-packed)

6 tablespoons lemon juice

1¼ cups plain, or Greek-
style (thick), yogurt

1 bunch of chives, snipped

Remove the mackerel skin and cut the fillets into very small pieces with a knife or, better, with sharp kitchen scissors.

Flatten the pieces with the back of a spoon.

Mix the lemon juice in a bowl with the yogurt and chives then add the mackerel.

Chill in the refrigerator until ready to serve.

Suggestion

This mackerel tartare makes a good appetizer served on slices of toasted baguette.

Marinated herring tartare

Serves 4

6 herring fillets (sold vacuum-packed)

2 onions, finely chopped

1 cup sour cream

1 large crisp eating apple (organic, if possible, to use the skin)

Chop the herring fillets finely (lengthwise or in squares).

Mix with the chopped onions and add the sour cream.

Just before serving, grate the unpeeled apple and add it to the mixture.

When the apple has been added, this tartare will keep in the refrigerator until the following day.

Serve it on toast.

Variation (see photograph)

The herring fillets could also be cut into strips and formed into rounds. Then add a dollop of sour cream and top with the finely chopped apple and chopped onion.

Mixed vegetable tartare

Serves 4

Serves 4

2 firm tomatoes

2 small zucchini

1 small cucumber

3 carrots

10 pink radishes

5 small cauliflower florets

5 small broccoli florets

1 stalk celery

1 scallion

For the dressing:

4 tablespoons lemon juice

1 teaspoon strong mustard

1 teaspoon Worcestershire sauce

$^2/_3$ cup plain yogurt

salt and freshly ground black pepper

4 small ramekins

Wash and dry all the vegetables carefully.

Dice them as finely as possible with a well-sharpened knife. (Leave the skin on the tomatoes, zucchini, and cucumber).

Mix together the diced vegetables in a salad bowl.

Mix together the dressing ingredients and pour over the vegetables.

Mix again and put into the ramekins. Chill in the refrigerator for 15 minutes. Unmold a ramekin onto each plate before serving.

Variation

Any kinds of vegetables can be used for this tartare. Season with fresh herbs according to the vegetables you choose.

Tomato, feta cheese, and basil tartare

Serves 4

1 lb cherry tomatoes

2 cups finely diced feta cheese

1 tablespoon olive oil

1 bunch of basil

salt

4 small ramekins

Wash and seed the cherry tomatoes. Cut in small pieces and divide among the ramekins.

Mix the olive oil and feta then add half the basil leaves. Feta is a salty cheese so check for taste before seasoning with salt.

Pour over the tomatoes and mix in.

Decorate with the remaining basil leaves and serve.

Suggestion

The feta could be replaced by ricotta or mozzarella.

Cucumber and dill tartare

Serves 4

2 cucumbers (organic if possible) unpeeled

1½ tablespoons white wine vinegar

2 shallots, finely chopped

6 tablespoons olive oil

4 artichoke hearts

2 firm tomatoes, seeded

8 dill sprigs

salt and freshly ground black pepper

Wash and dry the cucumbers.

Using a mandoline, slice one of the cucumbers, into very fine rounds. Put in a colander, sprinkle with salt and leave to drain for 20 minutes.

Quarter the second cucumber lengthwise. Remove the central core with the seeds and finely dice the rest.

Place in another colander, sprinkle with salt and leave to drain for 20 minutes.

In a bowl, mix the vinegar, shallots, and the olive oil. Season with salt and pepper.

Arrange the cucumber slices on plates in overlapping circles. Place an artichoke heart in the middle of each plate and pour over a teaspoon of the vinaigrette.

Finely chop the tomatoes and mix with the cucumber dice. Garnish each artichoke with the mixture.

Just before serving, pour the remaining vinaigrette over each plate and sprinkle with chopped dill.

Tartare of artichoke with tarragon

Serves 4

4 artichoke hearts

4 hearts of palm

14-oz piece mozzarella cheese

4 firm tomatoes

4 tablespoons olive oil

½ bunch tarragon

salt

4 small ramekins

Finely dice the artichoke hearts, hearts of palm, and mozzarella and mix together thoroughly in a bowl.

Seed the tomatoes and dice finely. Add to the bowl.

Mix together the olive oil, tarragon leaves, and salt to taste. Add to the bowl and mix well.

Divide the mixture among the ramekins, packing them firmly, then chill in the refrigerator for 15 minutes.

Just before serving, unmold onto 4 plates.

Suggestion

Basil can be used instead of tarragon, if you prefer. It also goes very well with mozzarella and tomato.

Tartare of minted peaches and pears

Serves 4

1 ripe white peach

3 tablespoons light brown soft sugar

a few mint leaves, chopped

2 tablespoons lemon juice

3 firm pears

2 firm yellow peaches

12 raspberries

4 small ramekins

Peel the white peach and purée with the sugar and the chopped mint leaves.

Pour the lemon juice over the mixture immediately.

Peel the pears and the yellow peaches and cut them into small pieces.

Pour the white peach and mint purée over the pears and yellow peaches and mix well.

Divide among the ramekins, pack down firmly, cover with plastic wrap and chill in the refrigerator until ready to serve.

To serve, unmold each ramekin onto a plate and decorate with sprigs of mint and a few raspberries.

Tartare of pineapple and mangoes with coconut milk

Serves 4

1 pineapple

4 mangoes

vanilla sugar or icing sugar, for dusting

1 cup coconut milk

oconut flakes, to decorate

Cut off the top and bottom of the pineapple and remove the skin.

Cut four large rounds from the middle of the pineapple and put one on each plate.

Finely dice the rest of the pineapple.

Cut the mangoes in half, running a knife around the nut to remove it. Take off the skin and finely dice the flesh.

Scatter the mango dice around each pineapple slice, reserving the equivalent of one mango.

Mix the remaining diced pineapple and mango and spoon onto the center of each pineapple round.

Dust each plate with vanilla sugar or icing sugar and sprinkle lightly with coconut milk.

Decorate with flaked coconut. Serve immediately.

Tartare of strawberries with basil

Serves 4

1/2 cup pine nuts

1 lb strawberries

½ eating apple

2 tablespoons lemon juice

8 basil leaves, plus 1 or 2 to decorate each ramekin

1 scant ½ cup olive oil

1½ tablespoons superfine sugar

zest of one unwaxed, or well-scrubbed lemon

Lightly toast the pine nuts in a pan, turning constantly.

Wash the strawberries and cut into small pieces.

Peel the half-apple and cut into small dice. Sprinkle over the lemon juice immediately, to prevent it discoloring.

Put the basil leaves, pine nuts, olive oil and sugar in a blender and process briefly.

Remove to a bowl. Add the strawberries and diced apple and stir gently.

Divide the mixture into ramekins, glasses, or plates. Decorate with basil leaves and the lemon zest.

Suggestion

You could also decorate with red berries such as red currants or raspberries.

Beef carpaccio

Serves 4

14 oz fillet of beef

4 tablespoons fruity olive oil

2 tablespoons lemon juice

$\frac{1}{2}$ cup Parmesan cheese shavings

4 basil sprigs

salt and freshly ground black pepper

For the pear variation

2 pears, peeled and sliced

For the marinade:

juice of $\frac{1}{2}$ orange

1 stick cinnamon

2 teaspoons light brown soft sugar

$\frac{1}{4}$ teaspoon cumin seeds

$\frac{1}{4}$ teaspoon pink peppercorns

$\frac{1}{4}$ teaspoon crushed cardamom seeds

zest of $\frac{1}{4}$ lemon

Wrap the fillet of beef in plastic wrap and freeze for 1 hour then unwrap and slice very finely with a well-sharpened knife. If the slices are not fine enough, put them between two pieces of plastic wrap and flatten gently with a rolling pin.

Arrange the slices on well-chilled plates.

Mix together the oil and lemon juice and brush over the strips of beef. Cover the plates with plastic wrap and refrigerate for 20 minutes.

When ready to serve, season the carpaccio with salt and pepper to taste, and add the Parmesan shavings.

Pour over the remaining oil and lemon juice and decorate with basil leaves.

Variation with pears (see photograph)

When you put the beef in the freezer mix together the ingredients for the pear marinade and steep the sliced pears in it.

Proceed as for the classic carpaccio up to the point when you take the plates from the refrigerator. Season the carpaccio and drizzle over the oil and lemon mixture.

Drain the pear slices and arrange between the slices of beef. Garnish with the lemon zest.

Serve immediately.

Carpaccio of duckling with oranges

Serves 4

4 small oranges (preferably organic)

2 smoked duckling breasts

juice of ½ orange

2 tablespoons lemon juice

1 teaspoon runny honey

1 teaspoon French mustard

4 tablespoons olive oil

1 teaspoon coriander seeds

1 teaspoon pink peppercorns

4 tarragon sprigs, to garnish

fleur de sel or fine sea salt, freshly ground black pepper

Wash, dry, and finely slice the oranges. Arrange the slices on 4 plates.

Cut the duckling breasts into very fine slices, carefully removing any traces of fat. Arrange the slices in a fan shape on the plates.

Mix together the orange and lemon juice, honey, mustard, and olive oil and brush over the slices of duckling. Trickle the remaining mixture around the plates.

Sprinkle with coriander seeds, pink peppercorns, salt, and pepper. Garnish with the tarragon sprigs.

Chill the plates in the refrigerator for 20 minutes before serving.

Veal carpaccio

Serves 4

14 oz fillet of veal

4 tablespoons olive oil

2 cloves garlic, crushed

1 teaspoon coriander seeds, cracked

1 teaspoon oregano

salt and freshly ground pepper

For the tuna variation

3½ oz canned tuna, in oil

Put the veal fillet in the freezer for 45 minutes.

At the same time, chill 4 plates in the refrigerator (for around 30 minutes).

Slice the veal fillets very finely and arrange on the cold plates. Brush with olive oil.

Sprinkle the meat with the crushed garlic, coriander seeds, and oregano.

Drizzle the remaining olive oil over each plate. Season to taste and serve immediately.

Variation with tuna

Scatter tuna flakes over the veal slices and continue as above.

Carpaccio of shrimp with cilantro and dill

Serves 4

12 gambas (large shrimp), very fresh

zest of 1 unwaxed, or well-scrubbed, lemon

4–5 cilantro sprigs, snipped

4–5 dill sprigs, snipped

juice of 2 limes

4 tablespoons olive oil

¾ cup flaked Parmesan cheese

salt and freshly ground black pepper

Peel the shrimp and cut them in half along their length. Take out the black 'vein'.

Put the shrimp halves on 4 plates. Sprinkle them with the lemon zest, cilantro and dill.

Chill the plates in the refrigerator for 30 minutes.

When ready to serve, pour over the lime juice and olive oil. Season, then sprinkle with Parmesan flakes.

Salmon carpaccio with ginger and lime

Serves 4

14 oz salmon fillet or steak, skinned and boned

1–2 inches fresh ginger, grated

juice of 2 limes

4 tablespoons olive oil

5 tablespoons light soy sauce (to serve)

salt

Freeze the salmon for 30 minutes to firm up the flesh.

Cut it into very fine slices and arrange on 4 plates.

Sprinkle with the grated ginger to taste, then pour over the lime juice and olive oil. Season to taste with salt.

Hand round the soy sauce separately.

Suggestion

Although the salmon is not served as sushi, the dressing used means it will go very well with rice, served with slices of baguette.

Tuna carpaccio with capers

Serves 4

14 oz fresh tuna

3 tablespoons capers

1 bunch of flat-leaf parsley, snipped

zest of ½ unwaxed, or well-scrubbed, lemon

8 tablespoons of lemon juice

5 tablespoons olive oil

salt and freshly ground pepper

Freeze the tuna for 30 minutes to firm the flesh.

When ready, cut it in very fine strips with a well-sharpened knife and arrange on 4 plates.

Sprinkle over the capers, parsley, and lemon zest. Pour over the lemon juice to taste.

Chill the plates in the refrigerator for 30 minutes.

When ready to serve, season with salt and pepper, followed by a drizzle of olive oil over each plate.

Suggestion

Arrange the tuna strips on a bed of oakleaf lettuce.

Carpaccio of salmon with lemon

Serves 4

14 oz salmon fillet

juice of 1 lemon

5 teaspoons olive oil

2 teaspoons soy sauce

½ cup pine nuts

½ cup Parmesan cheese shavings

5 oz mesclun or salad leaves

20 basil leaves, to garnish

salt and freshly ground black pepper

For the mushroom variation

10 oz button mushrooms

4 tablespoons sour cream

12 chive stalks, snipped

juice of 1 lime

Freeze the salmon fillet for 30 minutes to firm the flesh.

Cut into very fine slices and arrange on 4 plates.

Mix together the lemon juice, olive oil and soy sauce and pour over the salmon. Chill the plates in the refrigerator for 30 minutes.

Dry-fry the pine nuts in a nonstick pan, stirring constantly.

Sprinkle the plates with Parmesan shavings and toasted pine nuts.

Surround with the mesclun or salad leaves. Season with salt and pepper to taste, garnish with basil leaves and serve immediately.

Variation with mushrooms

Slice the mushrooms and sprinkle them with lime juice.

Take the salmon carpaccio from the refrigerator, where it has been macerating in its dressing, and add the mushroom slices to the plates.

Add a tablespoon of sour cream to each serving. Scatter over the chopped chives and Parmesan shavings.

Suggestion

This salmon carpaccio can be served as a substantial appetizer but you can easily turn it into a main dish by adding green vegetables or rice.

Carpaccio of scallops with chives

Serves 4

16 scallops

juice of 1 lime

4 tablespoons olive oil

1 teaspoon pink peppercorns

1 tablespoon snipped chives

¼ small red bell pepper, chopped

fleur de sel **or fine sea salt**

Freeze the scallops for 10 minutes to firm them.

Remove the roe (the orange part) if necessary and slice each scallop into fine strips.

Arrange them on the plates.

Mix together the dressing ingredients and pour over the scallops and around each dish. Serve immediately.

Suggestions

If you find lime juice a bit too sharp, you can substitute lemon juice.

A finely chopped shallot will enhance the flavor of this maritime dish.

Carpaccio of sea bass with fennel

Serves 4

1¼ lb fillet of sea bass

4 tablespoons lemon juice

5 tablespoons olive oil

¼ teaspoon dill seeds

1 clove garlic, crushed

1 tablespoon white wine

1 teaspoon white sugar

1 small fennel bulb

salt and white pepper

Wrap the sea bass in plastic wrap and freeze for 30 minutes.

Mix together the lemon juice, olive oil, dill seeds, garlic, white wine, and sugar. Season with salt and pepper to taste.

Remove the fish from the freezer and cut it into very thin slices. Arrange them on 4 plates.

Slice the fennel bulb into small pieces and arrange on the plates. Scatter the fennel leaves over the fish.

When ready to serve, pour the dressing mixture over the fish.

Suggestion

If fresh dill is available, use it instead of dill seeds.
Crushed aniseed also goes well with fennel.

Carpaccio of zucchini with toasted pine nuts

Serves 4

2 zucchini

½ pine nuts

½ cup Parmesan cheese shavings

4 tablespoons lemon juice

3 tablespoons olive oil

salt and freshly ground pepper

Slice the zucchini into very thin rounds with a mandoline set on the finest blade. Arrange the slices on plates.

Dry-fry the pine nuts in a nonstick pan, turning constantly. Scatter them over the zucchini.

Sprinkle the lemon juice over and chill the plates in the refrigerator for 30 minutes.

When ready to serve, season the zucchini with salt and pepper to taste and pour over the olive oil. Scatter over the Parmesan shavings.

Suggestions

Several snippets of chives added with the lemon juice will enhance the flavor of this dish.

For those who like it, garlic can also be added.

Carpaccio of mushrooms

Serves 4

1¼ lb button mushrooms

8 tablespoons of lemon juice

1 tablespoon balsamic vinegar

3 tablespoons olive oil

2 cloves garlic, chopped

2 tablespoons chopped parsley

salt and freshly ground pepper

Wipe the mushrooms. Remove the stalks, which can be used in another recipe such as a salad.

Slice the mushrooms very finely with a knife, or a mandoline if you have one.

Arrange the slices on plates and immediately pour over half of the lemon juice, to keep them from discoloring.

Mix together the balsamic vinegar, olive oil, remaining lemon juice to taste, the chopped garlic, and parsley.

Season with salt and pepper to taste and pour the vinaigrette over the carpaccio. Serve immediately.

Suggestion

This carpaccio makes a good appetizer.

Carpaccio of carrots with dates and feta cheese

Serves 4

5 large carrots

2 tablespoons balsamic vinegar

6 tablespoons olive oil

8-oz piece feta cheese

8 dates

3 shallots

salt

Peel the carrots with a swivel-blade vegetable peeler, if you have one.

When peeled, continue to shave each carrot into very thin strips, long or short as you prefer.

Mix together the balsamic vinegar, olive oil and a little salt. Trickle a tablespoonful around each plate.

Dice the feta and pile it in the center of each plate.

Arrange the carrot strips around the feta. If the strips are long, you could make them into flower shapes or, if short, simply scatter them.

Cut the dates into small pieces and finely chop the shallots. Scatter them over each plate.

Pour the remaining vinaigrette over the carrots or around each plate, if you prefer.

Suggestion

This carpaccio makes a good appetizer.

Cucumber and mint carpaccio

Serves 4

2 cucumbers

1¼ cups plain yogurt

2 cloves garlic, crushed

4 tablespoons olive oil

8 tablespoons lemon juice

3 or 4 mint sprigs, chopped
(set aside a few whole
leaves to garnish)

salt and freshly ground
black pepper

4 ramekins

Peel the cucumbers thinly.

Slice them into long thin strips, stopping before you reach the center and the seeds. Put the strips into a colander, sprinkle with salt, and let drain for around 20 minutes.

Whip the yogurt to obtain a smooth consistency. Add crushed garlic, olive oil, lemon juice to taste, and the chopped mint. Season with salt and pepper to taste.

Put this mixture in the bottom of the ramekins and arrange the cucumber strips on top in circles.

Chill in the refrigerator for 5 minutes.

Before serving, place several mint leaves on top of each dish.

Suggestion

This carpaccio makes a good appetizer or a refreshing accompaniment to a curry.

Apple carpaccio with chèvre cheese

Serves 4

5 crisp red eating apples

8 tablespoons lemon juice

½ cup pine nuts

2 rounds chèvre cheese

10 tablespoons runny honey

Wash, dry, quarter and core the apples, but do not peel. Cut them in thin slices.

Put the slices in a deep plate and pour over the lemon juice to prevent discoloration. Dry-fry the pine nuts in a nonstick pan, stirring constantly.

Cut the chèvre into thin slices.

Arrange the apple and cheese slices on 4 plates.

Warm the honey in a saucepan over a low heat, then pour over the apples and cheese. Sprinkle over the pine nuts.

Serve immediately.

Orange and chocolate carpaccio

Serves 4

5 oranges

1 tablespoon orange-flower water

juice of 2 oranges

3¹/₂ oz best-quality dark chocolate

For the honey variation

4 tablespoons runny honey

4 teaspoons olive oil

Peel the oranges, removing as much pith as possible, and cut in thin slices. Place in a deep plate.

Mix the orange-flower water with the orange juice and pour over the orange slices. Leave to marinate in the refrigerator for at least 1 hour.

Just before serving, melt the chocolate in a bowl set over a pan of barely simmering water.

Arrange the orange slices on 4 plates and pour over the marinade.

Pour over the melted chocolate.

This dessert can be prepared in advance (only the melted chocolate needs to be done at the last minute), which will enhance its flavor.

Variation with honey

When the orange slices have marinated in the orange juice and the orange-flower water, arrange them on each plate, leaving out the juice (you can use this as a refreshing drink).

Pour over each plate a tablespoonful of honey and a teaspoonful of olive oil. Serve immediately.

Grapefruit carpaccio

Serves 4

3 small grapefruit

½ cup light brown soft sugar

1 vanilla bean

1 large handful of red currants

For the exotic variation

2 teaspoons rum

½ cup pine nuts

2–3 mint sprigs

Peel the grapefruit, removing as much of the pith as possible, and slice into very thin rounds.

Arrange the rounds on each plate.

Sprinkle over the sugar, spreading it evenly to dissolve in the grapefruit juice. Refrigerate the plates for 10 minutes.

When ready to serve, split open the vanilla bean lengthwise and scrape out the inside with the tip of a knife to scatter the little seeds over each plate. Add the red currants.

Variation with pine nuts and rum

For a more exotic version, sprinkle the grapefruit slices with rum before adding the sugar.

Dry-fry the pine nuts and scatter over the grapefruit, together with a few leaves of fresh mint.

Melon and almond carpaccio

Serves 4

1 cup slivered almonds

2 small melons

4 tablespoons runny honey

1 tablespoon sweet fortified wine (port, sherry) or orange liqueur

4 small rosemary sprigs (or several basil or mint leaves)

For the mozzarella cheese variation

7-oz piece mozzarella

Brown the almonds gently in a pan for several minutes, stirring constantly.

Cut the melons in half and remove the seeds. Remove the skin and slice the fruit very thinly, or cut into dice.

Arrange the slices in a fan shape on 4 plates or divide the diced melon among 4 bowls. Drizzle a tablespoon of honey over the melon. Add several drops of fortified wine or orange liqueur and scatter over the almonds.

Decorate each plate with a rosemary sprig or with several basil or mint leaves.

Variation with mozzarella cheese

Add thin slices of mozzarella to the melon.

Accessories and equipment supplied by:

Habitat, Le Jacquard Français, Potiron.

Styling: Garlone Bardel

© Marabout 2003

text © Marie-Victoire Garcia.

photographs © Akiko Ida

© Hachette Livre (Hachette Pratique) 2003
This edition published by Hachette Illustrated UK, Octopus Publishing Group Ltd.,
2–4 Heron Quays, London E14 4JP

English translation by JMS Books LLP (email: moseleystrachan@blueyonder.co.uk)
Translation © 2004 Octopus Publishing Group

A CIP catalog for this book is available from the Library of Congress

ISBN: 1 84430 067 6

Printed by Tien Wah, Singapore